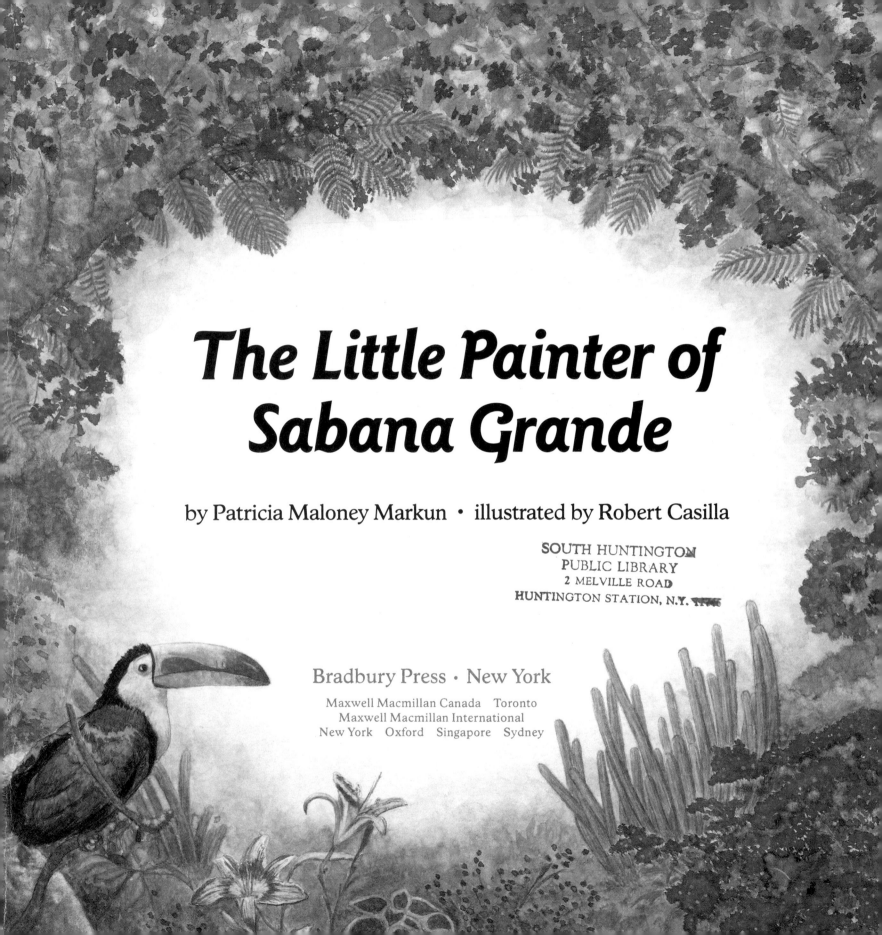

The Little Painter of Sabana Grande

by Patricia Maloney Markun · illustrated by Robert Casilla

Bradbury Press · New York

Maxwell Macmillan Canada   Toronto
Maxwell Macmillan International
New York   Oxford   Singapore   Sydney

J. Markun

Bradbury Press
Macmillan Publishing Company
866 Third Avenue
New York, NY 10022

Maxwell Macmillan Canada, Inc.
1200 Eglinton Avenue East
Suite 200
Don Mills, Ontario M3C 3N1

Macmillan Publishing Company is part of the Maxwell Communication
Group of Companies.

First American edition
Printed and bound in Hong Kong by South China Printing Company (1988) Ltd.
10 9 8 7 6 5 4 3 2 1
The text of this book is set in 14 point Stratford.
Book design by Julie Quan

LIBRARY OF CONGRESS CATALOGING-IN-PUBLICATION DATA
Markun, Patricia Maloney.
The little painter of Sabana Grande / by Patricia Maloney Markun.
p.   cm.
Summary: Lacking paper, a young Panamanian artist paints the
outside of his adobe home.
ISBN 0-02-762205-3
[1. Painting — Fiction. 2. Artists — Fiction. 3. Panama — Fiction.]
I. Title.   PZ7.M3288Li   1993
[E] — dc20   91-35230

For seven small painters: David, Eve,
Grace, Leslie, Sybil, Peter, and Luke.
And for three bigger ones: Brooke,
Zachary, and Richard
—PMM

For Robert, Jr., and Antonio
—RC

igh in the mountains of Panama lies the village of Sabana Grande. It is very small. Just seven houses of clay adobe stand alongside a brook in a grassy meadow. In the middle house lives the Espino family.

At dawn one cool purple morning, the rooster next door crowed. The Espinos woke up.

Papa went off to the meadow to milk the cow.

Mama stirred up the fire in the open-air kitchen and fried golden breakfast tortillas.

Fernando rolled up his straw sleeping mat and put it in the corner. He hurried to the kitchen to eat his tortilla right away.

This was an important day. At school Fernando had learned to draw colored pictures with crayons. Now school was out for dry-season vacation, and Fernando was going to paint for the first time.

His teacher, Señora Arias, had told him exactly how the country people of Panama made their paints. She said:

"Black from the charcoal of a burned tree stump.
Blue of certain berries that grow deep in the jungle.
Yellow from dried grasses in the meadow.
And red from the clay on the bottom of the brook."

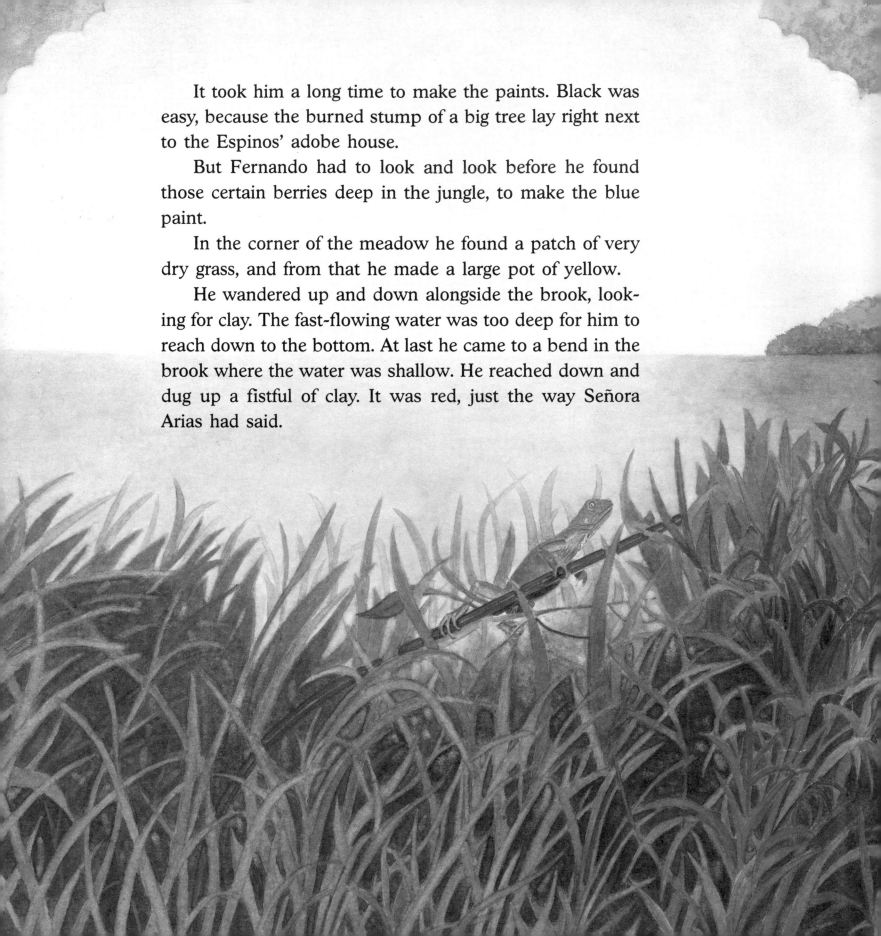

It took him a long time to make the paints. Black was easy, because the burned stump of a big tree lay right next to the Espinos' adobe house.

But Fernando had to look and look before he found those certain berries deep in the jungle, to make the blue paint.

In the corner of the meadow he found a patch of very dry grass, and from that he made a large pot of yellow.

He wandered up and down alongside the brook, looking for clay. The fast-flowing water was too deep for him to reach down to the bottom. At last he came to a bend in the brook where the water was shallow. He reached down and dug up a fistful of clay. It was red, just the way Señora Arias had said.

Now his paints were stirred up and waiting—black, blue, yellow, and red, in four bowls. Next he got out the three paintbrushes his teacher had given him—one very small, one medium-sized, and one especially large.

I'm ready to paint pictures, Fernando said to himself. He picked up the small brush and dipped it into the pot of red. Then he had a terrible thought.

He had nothing to paint a picture on! An artist needs paper.

He looked in both rooms of the house. He could find no paper at all.

He ran from house to house asking everyone in Sabana Grande for paper to paint on. None of the neighbors had any. Not a scrap.

Fernando was sad. After all his work he wouldn't be able to paint pictures—the colored pictures he could almost see, he wanted to make them so badly. Paints and brushes weren't enough. He needed paper, too.

His fingers itched to draw something—anything. He put down the paintbrush and went over to the mud by the brook. He picked up a stick and drew in the wet dirt, the way he had ever since he was a very little boy.

The big rooster who woke him every morning came out of the chicken yard next door. Fernando looked at him and drew the shape of a rooster. He sighed. He couldn't use his new red and yellow paints to make a bright rooster. He couldn't make the rooster's comb red. He could only scratch out a mud-colored rooster. It wasn't the same as painting would be. It didn't have any color.

Fernando looked around at the adobe houses of his village. Suddenly he got an idea. Adobe was smooth and white — almost like paper. Why couldn't he paint on the outside of his family's adobe house?

"No!" Papa said. "Who ever saw pictures on the outside of a house?"

"No!" Mama agreed. "What would the neighbors say?"

Fernando looked at his pots of paint and was very unhappy. He wanted to paint pictures more than anything else he could think of.

At last Papa said, "I can't stand to see my boy so miserable. All right, Fernando. Go ahead and paint on the house!"

Mama said, "Do your best, Fernando. Remember, the neighbors will have to look at your pictures for a very long time."

First Fernando made a tiny plan of the pictures he was going to paint, painting it with his smallest brush on one corner of the house.

"Your plan looks good to me, Fernando," Papa said. "If you can paint pictures small, you should be able to paint them big."

Fernando picked up his bigger brushes and started to paint a huge picture of the most beautiful tree in Panama, the flowering poinciana, on the left side of the front door. As he painted, he could look up and see the red flowers of a poinciana tree, just beginning its dry season, blooming on the mountainside.

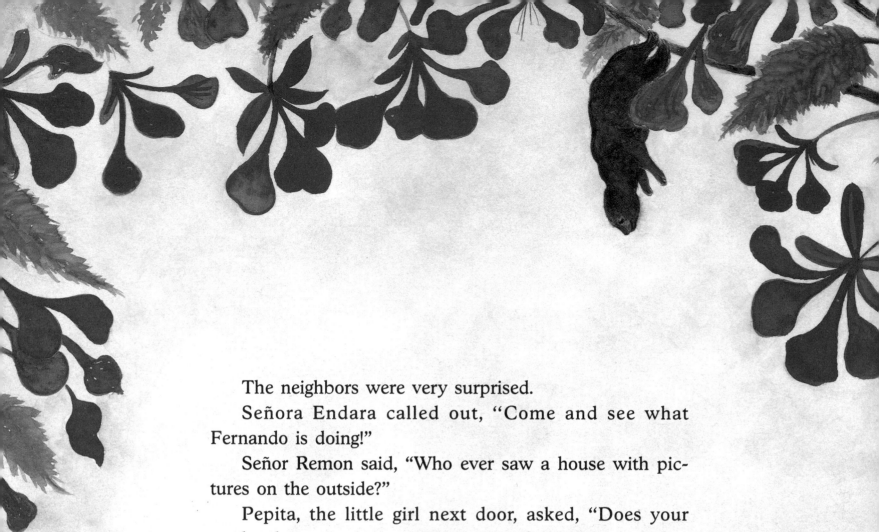

The neighbors were very surprised.

Señora Endara called out, "Come and see what Fernando is doing!"

Señor Remon said, "Who ever saw a house with pictures on the outside?"

Pepita, the little girl next door, asked, "Does your mother know you're painting on your house?"

Fernando nodded and smiled and kept on painting. Now and then he would look up at the mountain to see the real poinciana. After a week its flowers faded and died. Fernando's tree grew bigger and brighter and redder.

On one branch he added a black toucan with a flat, yellow bill. On another branch a lazy, brown sloth hung by its three toes.

The neighbors brought out chairs. While Fernando worked, they drank coffee and watched him paint.

Next he painted the wall on the other side of the door. An imaginary vine with flat, green leaves and huge, purple blossoms crept up the wall.

Word spread about the little painter of Sabana Grande. Even people from Santa Marta, the village around the mountain, hiked into town to watch him paint. The purple vine now reached almost to the thatched roof.

One day Señora Arias came from the school in Santa Marta. Why was his teacher looking for him, Fernando wondered. It was still dry season, when there wasn't any school. It hadn't rained for a month.

"School's not starting yet," his teacher said. "I came to see your painted adobe house that everyone in Santa Marta is talking about. Fernando, you did very well with those paintbrushes. I like it!"

She turned to the neighbors. "Don't you?"

"We certainly do!" the neighbors agreed.

They poured some coffee for the visiting teacher.

"Fernando, will you paint pictures on my house?" asked Señora Alfaro.

"And mine, too?" asked Señor Remon.

Fernando nodded yes, but he kept on painting.

For fun he added a black, white-faced monkey looking down at the people through purple flowers.

Next to the door he painted a big red-and-yellow rooster, flopping its red comb as it crowed a loud "cock-a-doodle-doo!"

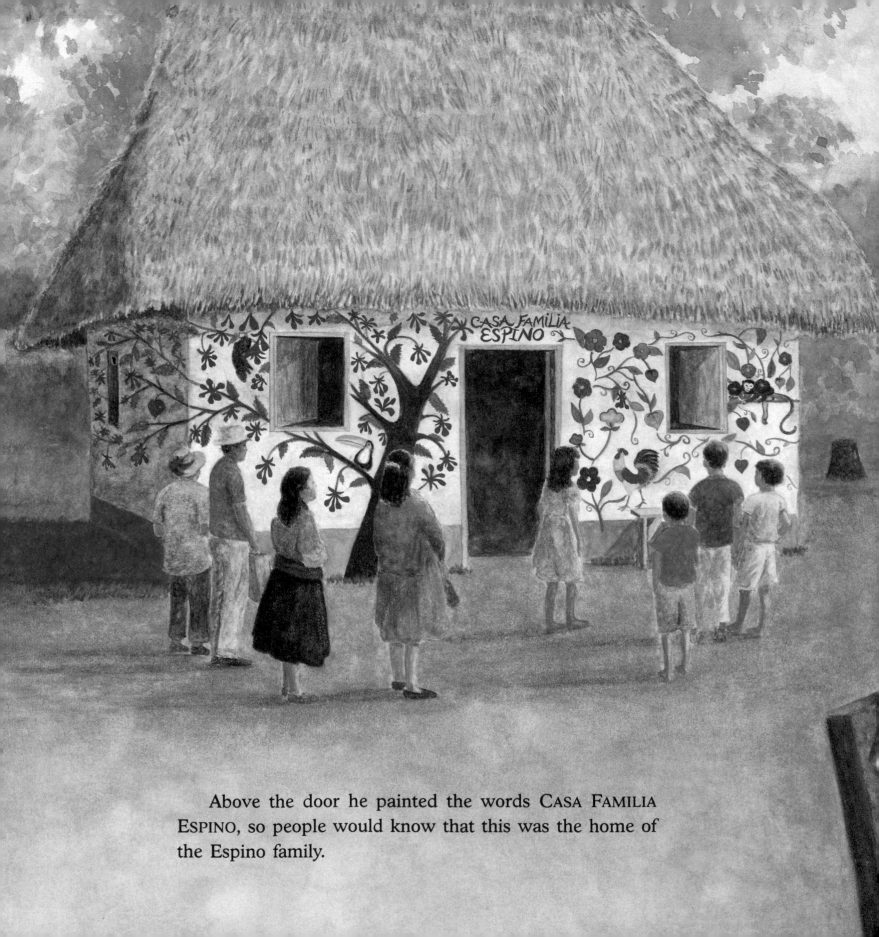

Above the door he painted the words CASA FAMILIA ESPINO, so people would know that this was the home of the Espino family.

Now his pictures were finished. Fernando sat down with his teacher and the neighbors. Everyone said kind words about his paintings.

Fernando said nothing. He just smiled and thought to himself, There are still six adobe houses left to paint in Sabana Grande.

Glossary of Central American Words

Adobe: Sun-dried brick made of clay

Casa Familia Espino: Spanish for "home of the Espino family"

Dry season: January, February, and March — the months
    when it doesn't rain — are the Panamanian summer and
    school vacation time.

Poinciana: A tropical tree with large red flowers

Sabana Grande: Spanish for "big meadow"

Tortilla: A pancake made of ground corn